Jimmy Carter:
A Life of Service and Conscience

James Earl Carter Jr., widely known as Jimmy Carter, was born on October 1, 1924, in Plains, Georgia, and was raised in the heart of a rural farming community. His father managed a general store, and his mother, a nurse, imparted not only care but also a sense of community awareness. Growing up mostly alongside African-American friends in his neighborhood, he was exposed to a diverse reality, fostering a sense of empathy that would shape his future endeavors.

After completing high school and two years of undergraduate coursework, Carter enrolled himself at the United States Naval Academy, graduating successfully in 1946. This marked the beginning of his naval career, which propelled him into submarine operations and allowed him to play a pivotal role in advancing nuclear propulsion technology. However, his father's passing in 1953 prompted his return to Georgia to oversee his family's peanut farm. Having struggled initially, he navigated the early obstacles by taking loans, and eventually managed to reverse the farm's fortune through his persistence and support from his wife, Rosalynn.

Carter's entry into politics began with his election to the Georgia State Senate in 1962. His progressive stance on civil rights and education reform set him apart, marking him as a thoughtful and dedicated legislator. Though a 1966 gubernatorial campaign fell short, the experience enriched his perspective and forged crucial connections.

Carter's political trajectory experienced an upward shift following his successful second gubernatorial campaign in 1970. While he initially embraced a more conservative stance during the election to resonate with the southern state's voters, his post-victory shift to a more liberal position surprised his supporters. As Georgia's 76th governor, he used his position to advocate for civil rights, enhance government efficiency, and enact budget reform. During his tenure, he appointed more women and minorities to state positions than any previous governor.

Carter's progressive policies resonated beyond Georgia's borders, drawing national attention and paving the way for his entry into the 1976 Democratic primary race. Against formidable odds, Carter emerged as the nominee, carrying a platform rooted in social justice, environmental protection, and government transparency.

Amidst the aftermath of the Nixon scandal, Carter's reformer stance resonated with the American public, leading to his victory in the 1976 election, subsequently making him the 39th President of the United States.

Presidential Years (1977 - 1981)

Carter's presidency was marked by a series of pivotal decisions and policies that aimed to address some key domestic and international challenges. His leadership during a time of economic uncertainty, energy crisis, and shifting global dynamics showcased his commitment to both national and international interests.

During his presidency, Carter grappled with the U.S. energy crisis, prompted by escalating oil prices and energy dependence concerns. He responded with a comprehensive energy policy emphasizing conservation, alternative energy sources, and reduced oil imports. Innovative measures like tax credits for energy-efficient technologies and investments in renewable energy research exemplified his commitment to a more sustainable energy future.

Carter's dedication to energy conservation was underscored by his personal actions, including installing solar panels on the White House roof and advocating simple practices such as wearing a sweater to conserve heating energy. Additionally, he established the U.S. Department of Energy in 1977, centralizing energy-related efforts and addressing long-term energy challenges with a comprehensive approach.

Carter saw healthcare and education as key to social progress. His administration pursued policies to expand healthcare access, including strengthening community health centers and enhancing preventive care. In education, Carter advocated for increased federal funding, focusing on equal opportunities for all students. He established the United States Department of Education and extended the Head Start program—an early childhood education initiative—to include migrant children, underscoring his commitment to inclusive learning.

Carter's presidency also oversaw notable deregulation initiatives, particularly in the airline and alcohol industries. Deregulation of the airline industry led to increased competition, lower fares, and improved consumer access to air travel.

Similarly, Carter's decision to lift federal restrictions on the production and sale of alcoholic beverages allowed for greater consumer choice and market competition, and also fostered a growth in home and microbrewing, contributing to a dynamic shift in the industry landscape.

During Carter's term, a prominent economic concern was stagflation, characterized by a blend of stagnant economic growth and high inflation. This formidable challenge persisted throughout his tenure, prompting his administration to adopt counterinflationary measures such as monetary tightening and wage-price guidelines. Despite these efforts, the outcomes revealed a mixed impact and underscored the intricate nature of the economic landscape during his presidency.

Foreign Policy Challenges and Achievements

One of the most significant achievements in Carter's foreign policy was the Camp David Accords of 1978. Under Carter's guidance, negotiations between Egyptian President Anwar Sadat and Israeli Prime Minister Menachem Begin resulted in a groundbreaking peace treaty. This historic achievement not only advanced stability in the region but also earned Carter international recognition, which – alongside his humanitarian work with the Carter Center – earned him the Nobel Peace Prize in 2002.

Carter's foreign policy also extended to the negotiation of the Strategic Arms Limitation Talks (SALT II) treaty, aimed at mitigating the arms race.

Despite being signed, the treaty encountered resistance in the U.S. Senate and was eventually withdrawn following the Soviet invasion of Afghanistan in 1979, straining diplomatic relations and hampering Carter's broader efforts toward détente.

Carter's engagement with Africa underscored his commitment to human rights and democratic governance. He staunchly opposed apartheid in South Africa and took an active role in facilitating negotiations that ultimately resulted in an agreement for Rhodesia's transition to an independent Zimbabwe. These efforts vividly demonstrated Carter's dedication to pursuing peaceful resolutions and fostering inclusive policies.

Moreover, Carter's administration achieved a significant breakthrough in U.S.-China relations by formalizing diplomatic ties with the People's Republic of China. This pivotal move laid the groundwork for expanded engagement between the two nations. Simultaneously, Carter's foreign policy agenda encompassed the reduction of U.S. forces stationed in South Korea, contributing to the easing of tensions on the Korean Peninsula and fostering a conducive environment for diplomatic solutions.

Demonstrating further diplomatic foresight, Carter's administration also negotiated the transfer of the Panama Canal to Panamanian control by the year 1999. This significant accord brought closure to a contentious chapter in U.S. history and underscored a steadfast commitment to honoring the sovereignty of other nations.

However, Carter's tenure also encountered a significant challenge in Iran. The Iranian Revolution of 1979 resulted in the seizure of the U.S. Embassy in Tehran and the subsequent hostage crisis. This complex and protracted ordeal tested Carter's diplomatic acumen and leadership as he worked tirelessly to secure the release of the American hostages. Unfortunately, their release was only achieved after Carter's presidency had concluded, casting a shadow over his foreign policy legacy.

Post-Presidential Work

Jimmy Carter's post-presidential years are a testament to his enduring commitment to service, diplomacy, and global progress. Far from being a mere footnote to his time in office, this period has become a defining chapter of Carter's legacy, marked by significant achievements and a tireless dedication to making a positive impact on the world.

After leaving the White House in 1981, Carter embarked on a journey that would see him emerge as a global statesman, a humanitarian advocate, and a respected mediator. At the heart of his post-presidential work was the establishment of the Carter Center in 1982, an institution that would serve as a platform for addressing some of the most pressing global challenges.

One of the pillars of the Carter Center's mission was the promotion of democracy and human rights. Carter's unwavering belief in the power of democratic governance as a tool for positive change drove the organization's engagement in election monitoring across the world. Over the years, the Carter Center actively monitored and assessed elections in more than 110 countries across 35+ nations.

Through careful observation and rigorous analysis, the Carter Center played a vital role in ensuring transparent and fair electoral processes, thereby contributing to the strengthening of democratic institutions and the safeguarding of political freedoms.

Carter's skills as a mediator, honed during his presidency, found new avenues for expression in his post-presidential years. He undertook diplomatic missions to some of the world's most challenging conflict zones, working tirelessly to bring opposing parties to the negotiation table. Carter's mediations in Sudan, North Korea, and other regions demonstrated his ability to bridge divides and facilitate dialogue, often leading to peaceful resolutions and an enduring commitment to reconciliation.

The Carter Center's profound impact on public health is exemplified by its efforts to combat diseases affecting vulnerable populations. Guided by Carter's hands-on approach, the organization played a pivotal role in almost eradicating Guinea worm disease and river blindness. Through innovative strategies and community engagement, the Center's work directly addressed health challenges at their core. Notably, it established a village-based healthcare system in thousands of African communities, providing essential services and empowering local populations. This initiative reflects Carter's commitment to equitable healthcare and leaves a lasting legacy of service and impact.

Carter's dedication to humanitarian causes extended beyond specific programs, encompassing a broad spectrum of issues.

From advocating for gender equality and mental health awareness to promoting peacebuilding and nuclear disarmament, Carter's influence was felt across a wide range of global challenges. His leadership in these areas served as a rallying point for collective action and increased awareness, contributing to the ongoing discourse on critical global issues.

Recognition and Legacy

Carter's post-presidential endeavors earned him widespread recognition and accolades. In 2002, he was awarded the Nobel Peace Prize for his tireless efforts in advancing peace, democracy, and human rights. This prestigious honor served as a testament to the profound impact of his work and the indelible mark he had left on the world.

Moreover, according to critics of his work and also by his own admission, Carter's post-presidential efforts proved to be more impactful and highly successful than his term as president. This achievement was partly attributed to the freedom he had to undertake meaningful initiatives and directly engage with people, a level of impact he found constrained during his presidency.

Jimmy Carter's legacy stands as a remarkable testament to the power of dedicated service, visionary leadership, and unwavering commitment to the betterment of humanity. His enduring contributions continue to inspire generations, reminding us that one individual's steadfast pursuit of positive change can shape a legacy that transcends the boundaries of time and leaves an indelible imprint on the world.

The test of a
government is not
how popular it is
with the powerful
and privileged few,
but how honestly and
fairly it deals with
the many who must
depend on it.

To gain viewers, the 24-hour
news channels have now come to
rely on reporting that often
dramatizes or exaggerates each
reported rumor or fact.
In addition, the more radical
presentations of information
or commentary have proven to
be most popular, so radio and
television programs, like
political alignments, have
tended toward extremes.

I have never been
happier, more
exhilarated, at peace,
rested, inspired, and
aware of the grandeur
of the universe and the
greatness of God than
when I find myself in a
natural setting not
much changed from the
way He made it.

We'll never know
whether something
new and wonderful is
possible unless we try.
Let's scratch our heads,
stretch our minds,
be adventurous!

Because of the heavy emphasis that was placed on Soviet-American competition, a dominant factor in our dealings with foreign countries became whether they espoused an anti-communist line. [Due to this], there were times when right-wing monarchs and military dictators were automatically immune from any criticism of their oppressive actions.

All artists speak from a special time and place, from a personal inner experience, and at their best, from a broader vision that transcends and enlarges the understanding of human beings, of themselves, of other human beings, and of the world in which they live.

Our commitment to
human rights must be
absolute, our laws
fair, our natural
beauty preserved;
the powerful must not
persecute the weak,
and human dignity
must be enhanced.

The experience of
democracy is like
the experience of
life itself --
always changing,
infinite in its
variety, sometimes
turbulent and all
the more valuable
for having been
tested by adversity.

Penalties against possession of a drug should not be more damaging to an individual than the use of the drug itself; and where they are, they should be changed. Nowhere is this more clear than in the laws against possession of marijuana in private for personal use.

Our decision about energy will test the character of the American people and the ability of the President and the Congress to govern this Nation. This difficult effort will be the moral equivalent of war, except that we will be uniting our efforts to build and not to destroy.

The awareness that
health is dependent
upon habits that we
control makes us the
first generation in
history that to a
large extent
determines its
own destiny.

According to Gandhi,
the seven sins are
wealth without work,
pleasure without
conscience, knowledge
without character,
commerce without
morality, science
without humanity,
worship without
sacrifice, and politics
without principle.

Solid wastes are the discarded leftovers of our advanced consumer society. This growing mountain of garbage and trash represents not only an attitude of indifference toward valuable natural resources, but also a serious economic and public health problem.

Any system of economics
is bankrupt if it sees
either value or virtue
in unemployment. We
simply cannot check
inflation by keeping
people out of work..

Let us learn together
and laugh together
and work together
and pray together,
confident that in the
end we will triumph
together in the
right.

In order for us human beings to commit ourselves personally to the inhumanity of war, we find it necessary first to dehumanize our opponents, which is in itself a violation of the beliefs of all religions. Once we characterize our adversaries as beyond the scope of God's mercy and grace, their lives lose all value.

One of the most basic principles for making and keeping peace within and between nations. . . is that in political, military, moral, and spiritual confrontations, there should be an honest attempt at the reconciliation of differences before resorting to combat.

We don't have any
problem finding
enough things to do;
the problem we have
is making sure we
don't overload
ourselves
inadvertently.

War may sometimes be a
necessary evil. But no
matter how necessary,
it is always an evil,
never a good. We will
not learn how to live
together in peace by
killing each other's
children.

And I'm asking you for your good and for your nation's security to take no unnecessary trips, to use carpools or public transportation whenever you can, to park your car one extra day per week, to obey the speed limit, and to set your thermostats to save fuel. Every act of energy conservation like this is more than just common sense-I tell you it is an act of patriotism.

I think with the advent of Reagan, and subsequently, both parties, there's been a strong move towards the advantage given to the richer people, in taxation and grants and supplements and things of that kind. Primarily exacerbated more recently by the Supreme Court's stupid ruling on Citizens United, and now there's a massive flood of money into the political system that I think has subverted the essence of a moral and ethical standard that used to permeate American democracy. Now it's not an admirable process. I think we've gone backwards.

We cannot be both
the world's leading
champion of peace
and the world's
leading supplier of
the weapons of war.

To be true to
ourselves, we must
be true to others.

The relationship between
government and art must
necessarily be a delicate
one. It would not be
appropriate for the
government to try to
define what is good or
what is true or what is
beautiful. But government
can provide nourishment
to the ground within
which these ideas spring
forth from the seeds of
inspiration within the
human mind.

We have a tendency to condemn people who are different from us, to define their sins as paramount and our own sinfulness as being insignificant.

Two centuries ago our
nation's birth was a
milestone in the long
quest for freedom, but
the bold and brilliant
dream which excited
the founders of our
nation still awaits
its consummation.
I have no new dream
to set forth today,
but rather urge a fresh
faith in the old dream.

God gives us the
capacity for choice.
We can choose to
alleviate suffering.
We can choose to work
together for peace.
We can make these
changes -- and we
must.

When combined, the
small individual
contributors of
caring, friendship,
forgiveness, and
love, each of us
different from our
next-door neighbors,
can form a phalanx,
an army, with great
capability.

History teaches, perhaps, very few clear lessons. But surely one such lesson learned by the world at great cost is that aggression, unopposed, becomes a contagious disease.

We cannot resort to
simplistic or extreme
solutions which
substitute myths
for common sense.

The bond of our
common humanity
is stronger than the
divisiveness of our
fears and prejudices.

A strong nation, like a strong person, can afford to be gentle, firm, thoughtful, and restrained. It can afford to extend a helping hand to others. It's a weak nation, like a weak person, that must behave with bluster and boasting and rashness and other signs of insecurity.

A country will have
authority and influence
because of moral factors,
not its military strength;
because it can be humble
and not blatant and
arrogant; because our
people want to serve
others and not dominate
others. And a nation
without morality will
soon lose its influence
around the world.

Everyone who has run knows that its most important value is in removing tension and allowing a release from whatever other cares the day may bring.

The best way to enhance freedom in other lands is to demonstrate here that our democratic system is worthy of emulation.

We should live our lives as though Christ were coming this afternoon.

In many courts, plea bargaining serves the convenience of the judge and the lawyers, not the ends of justice, because the courts simply lack the time to give everyone a fair trial.

The existing and long-standing use of the word 'evolution' in our state's textbooks has not adversely affected Georgians' belief in the omnipotence of God as creator of the universe. There can be no incompatibility between Christian faith and proven facts concerning geology, biology, and astronomy. There is no need to teach that stars can fall out of the sky and land on a flat Earth in order to defend our religious faith.

Except during my childhood, when I was probably influenced by Michelangelo's Sistine Chapel depiction of God with a flowing white beard, I have never tried to project the Creator in any kind of human likeness. The vociferous debates about whether God is male or female seem ridiculous to me. I think of God as an omnipotent and omniscient presence, a spirit that permeates the universe, the essence of truth, nature, being, and life. To me, these are profound and indescribable concepts that seem to be trivialized when expressed in words.

The most serious and
universal problem is the
growing chasm between
the richest and poorest
people on earth. Citizens
of the ten wealthiest
countries are now
seventy-five times
richer than those who
live in the ten poorest
ones, and the separation
is increasing every year,
not only between nations
but also within them.

Human identity is no
longer defined by what
one does, but by what
one owns. But we've
discovered that owning
things and consuming
things does not satisfy
our longing for
meaning. We've learned
that piling up material
goods cannot fill the
emptiness of lives
which have no
confidence or
purpose.

I want to make it
clear, if there is ever
a conflict [between
environmental quality
and economic growth],
I will go for beauty,
clean air, water,
and landscape.

The basic issue is
whether America
will provide global
leadership that springs
from the unity and the
integrity of the American
people, or whether
extremist doctrines,
the manipulation of the
truth, will define
America's role in the
world. At stake is
nothing less than
our nation's soul.

Americans long thought that nature could take care of itself—or that if it did not, the consequences were someone else's problem. As we know now, that assumption was wrong; none of us is a stranger to environmental problems.

An unfortunate result of
the need for constant
reporting--especially on
Internet news outlets--
has been the demise of
hundreds of newspapers
that have proved unable
to compete, leaving major
cities and towns with one
merged journal, or, in
some cases, none at all.
The free and vigorous
presentation of different
opinion has been
sacrificed to
polarized uniformity.

Faith implies a
continuing search,
not necessarily a
final answer.

We must adjust to
changing times
and still hold
to unchanging
principles.

Nearly all inmates are drawn from the ranks of the powerless and the poor. A child of privilege frequently receives the benefit of the doubt; a child of poverty seldom does.

Acknowledging the physical realities of our planet does not mean a dismal future of endless sacrifice. In fact, acknowledging these realities is the first step in dealing with them. We can meet the resource problems of the world — water, food, minerals, farmlands, forests, overpopulation, pollution — if we tackle them with courage and foresight.

Like music and art,
love of nature is a
common language
that can transcend
political or social
boundaries.

Too many of us now
tend to worship self
indulgence and
consumption.

A fundamentalist can't bring himself or herself to negotiate with people who disagree with them because the negotiating process itself is an indication of implied equality.

We live in a time of
transition, an uneasy era
which is likely to endure for
the rest of this century...
During this period we may be
tempted to abandon some of
the time-honored principles
and commitments which have
been proven during the
difficult times of past
generations. We must never
yield to this temptation. Our
American values are not
luxuries but necessities –
not the salt in our bread
but the bread itself.

I think doctors care very deeply about their patients, but when they organize into the AMA, their responsibility is to the welfare of doctors, and quite often, these lobbying groups are the only ones that are heard in the state capitols and in the capitol of our country.

Because we are now
running out of gas
and oil, we must
prepare quickly for
a third change, to
strict conservation
and to the use of ...
permanent renewable
energy sources, like
solar power.

We deny personal
responsibility when we
plant landmines and, days
or years later, a stranger
to us — often a child - is
crippled or killed. From a
great distance, we launch
bombs or missiles with
almost total impunity, and
never want to know the
number or identity of the
victims.

(speaking of the inhumanities of war
— Nobel Lecture, December 10, 2002)

We know that a
peaceful world
cannot long exist
one-third rich and
two-thirds hungry.

Ninety percent of
our lawyers serve
10 percent of our
people. We are
over-lawyered and
under-represented.

With massive arsenals still on hair-trigger alert, a global holocaust is just as possible now, through mistakes or misjudgments, as it was during the depths of the Cold War.

My life since the White House has been much more all-encompassing, much more enjoyable. The main thing that I've acquired in the last twenty-seven years has been access to the poorest and most destitute, forgotten, and suffering people on Earth. It's not possible for a President to actually know them. But [now] we go into the remote areas of Africa, Latin America, and Asia, and actually meet with people who are suffering and find out why. Then we try to work with them, giving them maximum responsibility for correcting their own problems. So that's the element that's been most beneficial to me.

Because [grandparents] are usually free to love and guide and befriend the young without having to take daily responsibility for them, they can often reach out past pride and fear of failure and close the space between generations.

I don't believe that
China, in my lifetime
or maybe my children's
lifetime, be equal to
the United States
militarily speaking,
but they are very
careful to avoid any
engagement in war, they
are basically a peaceful
country, which gives
them another advantage
over the United States
when we are much more
inclined to go to war
for various reasons.

When I reflect upon my
blessings during my
very nice lifetime,
I am inspired to make
sure that I spend the
balance of the days of
my existence in a
productive way.

To me, Faith is not
just a noun but
also a verb.

I have come to realize
that in every person
there is something
fine and pure and
noble, along with a
desire for self-
fulfillment.

One of the most serious
problems that our
country has inherited
an unwillingness to
talk to anyone who
disagrees with us or
who won't accept,
before a discussion,
all the premises
that we demand.

In the life of the human spirit, words are action, much more so than many of us realize who live in countries where freedom of expression is taken for granted...The proof is that words are precisely the action for which dissidents in those countries are being persecuted.

We've got to stop
crying and start
sweating, stop
talking and start
walking, stop cursing
and start praying.
The strength we need
will not come from
the White House, but
from every house
in America.

It's abominable, and
it's a disgrace to a
great democracy...the
enormous infusion of
high quantities of
money to campaigns –
governors, Congress,
president and the
U.S. Senate.

There's always an element of self delusion among people who believe they ought to be President. There's an underestimation of your opponent and an overestimation of your own abilities. This is compatible with being rich and powerful, the idea that we were blessed by God because we deserve to be blessed.

Every advance in this half-century -- Social Security, civil rights, Medicare, aid to education, one after another -- came with the support and leadership of American Labor. You have represented all the people, not just your members. You have been the voice of forgotten people everywhere.

The proper function
of a government is
to make it easy for
people to do good
and difficult for
them to do evil.

If any agreement
between two nations
is to last, it must
serve the best
interests of
both nations.

Aside from the humanitarian aspects, it is well known that, under excruciating torture, a prisoner will admit almost any suggested crime. Such confessions are, of course, not admissible in trials in civilized nations.

We become not a
melting pot but a
beautiful mosaic.
Different people,
different beliefs,
different yearnings,
different hopes,
different dreams.

We have seven and a half
times as many people in
prison. And we have eight
times as many black women
in prison now as we did
in 1981, when I left the
White House. So that's
been one of the major
concerns I've had as a
non-lawyer, to criticize
the American justice
system, which is highly
biased against black
people and poor people.
And it still is.

This view that women
are somehow inferior to
men is not restricted to
one religion or belief.
It is widespread. Women
are prevented from
playing a full and
equal role in many
faiths.

I've never won an
argument with my wife;
and the only time I
thought I had I found
out the argument wasn't
over yet.

(Of his wife Rosalynn,
Reader's Digest March 1979)

Thoughtful criticism and close scrutiny of all government officials by the press and the public are an important part of our democratic society.

What are the things
that you can't see
that are important?
I would say justice,
truth, humility,
service, compassion,
love...They're the
guiding lights
of a life.

We are of course a
nation of differences.
Those differences don't
make us weak. They're
the source of our
strength...The
question is not when
we came here...but why
our families came
here. And what we did
after we arrived.

Now as in our past,
only the understanding
and involvement of the
people through full
and open debate can
help to avoid serious
mistakes and assure the
continued dignity and
safety of the nation.

The Social Security program is a pact between workers and their employers that they will contribute to a common fund to ensure that those who are no longer part of the work force will have a basic income on which to live. It represents our commitment as a society to the belief that workers should not live in dread that a disability, death, or old age could leave them or their families destitute.

Many of the most highly
publicized events of
my presidency are not
nearly as memorable or
significant in my life
as fishing with my
daddy.

When the laws
are written and
administered by the
most powerful leaders
in a society, it is
human nature for them
to understand, justify,
and protect the
interests of themselves
and people like them.
Many injustices arise
from this natural
human failing.

To work for better understanding among people, one does not have to be a former president sitting at a fancy conference room table. Peace can be made in the neighborhoods, the living rooms, the playing fields, and the classrooms of our country.

I never really had
any affinity for
politics. I've always
looked on politics as
a means to an end...
It has never been a
natural part of my
life.

Although American
medical skill is among
the best in the world, we
have an abominable system
in this country for the
delivery of health care,
with gross inequities
toward the poor--
particularly the working
poor--and profiteering
by many hospitals and
some medical doctors, who
prey on the vulnerability
of the ill.

If you fear making
anyone mad, then you
ultimately probe for
the lowest common
denominator of human
achievement.

Whether the borders
that divide us are
picket fences or
national boundaries,
we are all neighbors
in a global community.

I believe that anyone can be successful in life, regardless of natural talent or the environment within which we live. This is not based on measuring success by human competitiveness for wealth, possessions, influence, and fame, but adhering to God's standards of truth, justice, humility, service, compassion, forgiveness, and love.

The **truth is that male religious leaders have had - and still have - an option to interpret holy teachings either to exalt or subjugate women. They have, for their own selfish ends, overwhelmingly chosen the latter.**

Some devout Christians
are among the most fervent
advocates of the death
penalty, contradicting
Jesus Christ and justifying
their belief on an erroneous
interpretation of Hebrew
Scriptures. "An eye for an
eye, and a tooth for a tooth,"
their most likely response,
overlooks the fact that this
was promulgated by Moses as
a limitation- a prohibition
against taking both eyes or
all of an offender's teeth in
retribution.

Today, in directly harnessing the power of the Sun, we're taking the energy that God gave us, the most renewable energy that we will ever see, and using it to replace our dwindling supplies of fossil fuels.

Failure is a reality; we all fail at times, and it's painful when we do. But it's better to fail while striving for something wonderful, challenging, adventurous, and uncertain than to say, "I don't want to try because I may not succeed completely."

This discrimination
[against women],
unjustifiably attributed
to a Higher Authority,
has provided a reason or
excuse for the deprivation
of women's equal rights
across the world for
centuries...It also costs
many millions of girls and
women control over their
own bodies and lives, and
continues to deny them
fair access to education,
health, employment and
influence within their
own communities.

We have the heaviest concentration of lawyers on Earth—one for every five-hundred Americans...We have more litigation, but I am not sure that we have more justice. No resources of talent and training in our own society, even including the medical care, is more wastefully or unfairly distributed than legal skills.

I think the most
challenging thing
for me in my life and
in the Bible is that
we worship Jesus as
the Prince of Peace.
And America is
constantly at war.

Each of us must
rededicate ourselves to
serving the common good.
We are a community.
Our individual fates
are linked; our futures
intertwined; and if we
act in that knowledge and
in that spirit together,
as the Bible says: "We can
move mountains."

America did not
invent human rights.
In a very real sense
human rights
invented America.

Always tell the truth,
and take an interest
in serving the people
around you as much as
possible.

We simply must
balance our demand
for energy with our
rapidly shrinking
resources. By acting
now we can control
our future instead of
letting the future
control us.

The stronger the ties
that bind us to God,
the more likely we are
to live, react, and
behave in harmony
with...greater joy,
peace, and happiness.

I would describe
fundamentalism as, first
of all, a movement led
almost invariably by
authoritarian males who
consider themselves to be
superior to others and
who have an overwhelming
commitment to subjugate
women and to dominate
their fellow believers.

I think there ought to
be a strict separation
or wall built between
our religious faith
and our practice of
political authority
in office. I don't think
the President of the
United States should
extoll Christianity
if he happens to be a
Christian at the
expense of Judaism,
Islam or other faiths.

Formerly admired almost universally as the preeminent champion of human rights, the United States now has become one of the foremost targets of respected international organizations concerned about these basic principles of democratic life. Some of our actions are similar to those of abusive regimes that we have historically condemned.

There is a strong
religious commitment
to the sanctity of
human life, but,
paradoxically, some
of the most fervent
protectors of
microscopic stem
cells are the most
ardent proponents
of the death penalty.

Wherever life takes us, there are always moments of wonder.

Communicating our questions, hopes, and fears in prayer makes them—even to ourselves—more open and clear.

In the final analysis,
true justice is not a
matter of courts and
law books, but of a
commitment in each of
us to liberty and
mutual respect.

9 798861 384704